PRESENTED TO

_____

BY

_____

ON THIS DATE

Same Kind of Different As Me

RAILROAD CROSSING

As Me

FOR KIDS

written & illustrated by

RON HALL & DENVER MOORE

Authors of *Same Kind of Different As Me*

Previously published as *Everybody Can Help Somebody*

Tommy NELSON

A Division of Thomas Nelson Publishers

♥ I would like to dedicate this to my four granddaughters,
Griffin, Sadie, Kendall, and Whitney, who loved Denver and his stories.

And to Denver, to whom all children were precious.

Published in Nashville, Tennessee, by Tommy Nelson. Tommy Nelson is an imprint of Thomas Nelson. Thomas Nelson is a registered trademark of HarperCollins Christian Publishing, Inc.

Tommy Nelson titles may be purchased in bulk for educational, business, fund-raising, or sales promotional use. For information, please e-mail SpecialMarkets@ThomasNelson.com.

Scripture quotations are taken from the Holy Bible, New International Version®, NIV®. Copyright © 1973, 1978, 1984 by Biblica, Inc.® Used by permission of Zondervan. All rights reserved worldwide. www.zondervan.com. The "NIV" and "New International Version" are trademarks registered in the United States Patent and Trademark Office by Biblica, Inc.®

ISBN: 978-0-7180-9179-8

Library of Congress Cataloging-in-Publication Data

Names: Hall, Ron, 1945- author. | Moore, Denver author.
Title: Same kind of different as me for kids / written and illustrated by Ron
   Hall & Denver Moore, authors of Same kind of different as me.
Other titles: Everybody can help somebody
Description: Nashville : Thomas Nelson, 2017. | Originally published under
   title: Everybody can help somebody : Nashville : Tommy Nelson, 2013.
Identifiers: LCCN 2016030883 | ISBN 9780718091798 (hardcover)
Subjects: LCSH: Moore, Denver--Juvenile literature. | Homeless
   men--Texas--Fort Worth--Biography--Juvenile literature. | African
   Americans--Texas--Fort Worth--Biography--Juvenile literature. | Christian
   biography--Texas--Fort Worth--Juvenile literature. | Fort Worth
   (Tex)--Biography--Juvenile literature.
Classification: LCC F394.F7 H154 2017 | DDC 976.4/5315063092 [B] --dc23 LC record available at
https://lccn.loc.gov/2016030883

Printed in China

17 18 19 20 21 LEO 6 5 4 3 2 1

Mfr: LEO / Heshan, China / January 2017 / PO #9410484

He who is kind to the poor lends to the LORD,

and he will reward him for what he has done.

Proverbs 19:17

Dear parents,

For nearly ten years Denver and I traveled across America telling our story and hoping to make a difference in the way people view and treat the homeless. From the beginning it was evident that children were drawn to Denver.

After a six-year-old boy heard the story from *Same Kind of Different As Me* about how Denver never had a real toy as a child, he told his mother, "I want to give Denver my red fire truck." A few days later, the boy presented his favorite toy to Denver. Denver displayed that little red fire truck—and the kindness it represented—in a glass box like a great work of art until his passing.

Denver loved children, and his story moved many kids to action. "We gots to write a book these little children can read!" Denver told me. We finished this book shortly before Denver left earth to join Miss Debbie in heaven. This wise and godly man had these final words for the children: "Tell them nobody can help everybody, but everybody can help somebody!"

Denver's dream and my hope is that through the pages of this book, your children will be filled with compassion and with the desire to make a difference in the world around them by helping somebody.

Sincerely,
Ron Hall

"I used to spend a lotta time worryin'
that I was different from other people. . . .
But I found out everybody's different—
the same kind of different as me."

Not too many years ago, American people were struggling. That time was called the Great Depression. Families didn't have much money. Mothers and fathers couldn't find jobs to buy food, medicine, or warm clothes for their children.

That was the time when Denver was born, on a cold January day on a cotton plantation in Louisiana. He was so small that his granddaddy would carry him in the front pocket of his overalls.

Denver's family worked as sharecroppers picking cotton on The Man's plantation. The Man let them live in a shack on the plantation. They had no electricity. They had no lights. They had no water. They were as poor as they could be.

Denver's family didn't have a car. Sometimes they rode on a big wagon pulled by mules. But they usually walked.

Most of the food they ate came from their garden—corn, potatoes, carrots. The milk came from The Man's cow. At Christmas, The Man would give them a pig so they would have some meat.

Even though he was a little boy, Denver worked with the rest of his family. He fed the chickens. He milked the cows. He picked wild blueberries.

There wasn't money for toys, so Denver would make toy trucks from old boards, with bottle caps for the wheels.

One day, Denver saw The Man's son Bobby riding down the dirt road on a brand-new bicycle. It was shiny and red! Denver had never seen a bicycle. He wanted one so much! He asked The Man, "Can I do extra chores for you so I can earn enough money to buy a bike like Bobby's?"

"Denver," The Man said, "if you pick one hundred pounds of cotton, I will buy you a new bike."

Denver got up before the sun even came up the next morning and picked cotton all day, sweat trickling down his forehead and into his eyes. Just as the sun was setting, he took his pillowcase full of cotton to The Man's barn and put it on the scales. It only weighed five pounds!

Day after day, he worked in the hot sun and picked cotton until his hands and knees were so sore and swollen that he could not pick any more. The Man's son Bobby felt sorry for Denver and thought, *I'll pick some cotton too and sneak it into Denver's sack in the barn.* With a friend helping him, Denver finally had one hundred pounds of cotton.

A few days later, The Man said, "I have a surprise for you, Denver. Come with me and Bobby down to the barn." When they got to the barn, Denver swung the big doors open. Inside was a brand-new bike, just for him! It was shiny and red with a rubber horn on the handlebars. Denver couldn't believe his eyes.

"Oh, thank you! *Thank you!* THANK YOU!" he hollered loud enough for everyone on the plantation to hear. He gave The Man a big hug, and then he and Bobby rode off together on their bikes. It was the happiest day of Denver's life.

Most kids go to school, but not Denver. He had to work in the cotton fields instead. He wanted to learn to read and write his name, but nobody in Denver's family knew how to teach him.

Year after year, when the other kids headed off to school with their lunches and books, Denver stayed behind to work on the plantation. He picked the cotton, milked the cows, and fed the pigs and chickens.

Denver wasn't very happy. He wanted to learn and to see new places and to have enough money to buy things of his own. But all that sharecroppers like Denver could do was stay on the farm and work.

One day, when Denver was grown, he was walking to The Man's store and saw a train stopped on the railroad tracks. *I wonder where that train goes?* Denver thought. He decided to jump on the train and find out. He was ready to see the world.

Click, clack! Click, clack! The train sped along the tracks, all day and all night. Denver rode in a boxcar that carried coal. He got covered in coal dust. Soon his pretty brown skin looked as black as the coal. When the train finally stopped, Denver climbed down to the ground. He was in Fort Worth, Texas.

"What a big place!" Denver said as he walked through the city looking up at all the tall buildings. There were shops everywhere and people walking very fast in every direction. Everyone he saw wore nice clothes and looked all clean and shiny. Denver was barefoot and wearing overalls covered in coal dust. He didn't need a mirror to know that he did not look like anyone else in this town.

Denver had no money. He had no place to sleep. First, he dug through the trash cans near a restaurant for food. Then he slept in a cardboard box in the bushes under a bridge. He took a bath in the river.

Denver tried to get a job in a store, but he didn't know how to read or write his name on the application.

"Are you a homeless man?" the store owner asked. Denver didn't know what that meant. He'd never owned a home, but The Man had given him a shack to live in. Now his home was a cardboard box.

People weren't very nice to Denver. They wouldn't talk to him. They pretended they didn't see him. They said he was dirty and smelled bad and ate from garbage cans. No one would help him.

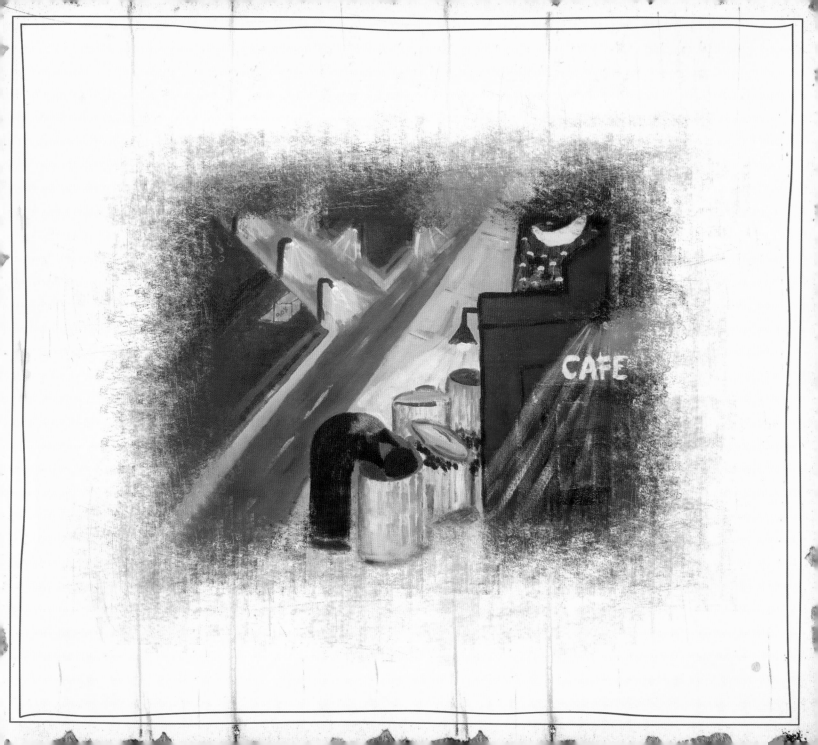

Denver spent a long time living as a homeless man. Being lonely, poor, and hungry made him mean.

He slept outside under bridges, on park benches, or near the front steps of churches. He hoped some of the nice church-goin' people would help him or give him some food—maybe a sandwich or a hot cup of coffee on a really cold day. But no one ever did.

No one cares about me, he thought. At night, he would look up at the sky full of stars. *Is there really a God up there?* he wondered. *Does He love me?*

There is a God. And He did love Denver. So He made a
very strange thing happen. A nice lady named Miss Debbie had
a dream about a homeless man. "I saw his face," Debbie told
her husband, Ron. "I saw a wise man who changed the city.
Let's see if we can find the man in my dream."

Debbie and Ron searched everywhere, but they couldn't find
the man in Debbie's dream.

Miss Debbie and Ron went every week to help at a homeless
mission. They gave out food and clothes. They also taught
homeless people how to read and write so they could get jobs.

One night, as Ron and Miss Debbie served dinner at the mission, she saw the man from her dream! "What's your name?" she asked.

"My name is Denver. I am a very bad man. Leave me alone!"

But Miss Debbie wasn't afraid. "You are not a bad man," she said softly. "You are a *good* man. God loves you, and so do I."

Denver had never heard anyone say, "God loves you." He had never even heard someone say, "I love you." Her words made him feel less angry and lonely. That night, as he lay in his cardboard box, he thought about the nice lady with the kind voice. *Is she an angel?* he wondered.

Denver and Miss Debbie became friends. She told him about God. She taught him how to read and write. Ron taught Denver how to paint pictures. He took Denver to art museums. They became friends.

Pretty soon, Denver started to feel happy. He knew that he would never be alone again. God would always be with him.

I am not a bad man, he thought. *I am a good man. God loves me. God made me. God gave me friends.*

Denver was so thankful that Miss Debbie and Ron loved him that he wanted to help other homeless people too. Denver and Ron traveled all across America asking everyone to help the homeless people in their cities.

People read about Denver in the newspapers. They saw him on TV. He was even invited to the White House to meet the president!

Denver told people about living in the cardboard box in the bushes under the bridge. He said that no one had ever loved him until Miss Debbie and Ron and that they had introduced him to God and His love.

"Miss Debbie was different from anybody I had ever met, and I was different from anybody she had ever met. But"—he said with a big smile—"I finally figured out that she was the *same kind of different as me.*"

nobody can help
everybody but everybody
can help somebody

Denver had learned that nobody can help everybody, but everybody can help somebody. And he wanted to spend the rest of his life helping as many somebodies as he could.

The next time you see a homeless person or a poor person, think of Denver. Remember how he was able to change his life because Miss Debbie was kind to him and said, "God loves you, and so do I."

You can help somebody too.